WORLD COMMODITIES

Coffee

GARRY CHAPMAN » GARY HODGES

This edition first published in 2011 in the United States of America by Smart Apple Media.

Smart Apple Media
P.O. Box 3263
Mankato, MN, 56002

First published in 2010 by
MACMILLAN EDUCATION AUSTRALIA PTY LTD
15–19 Claremont Street, South Yarra 3141

Visit our web site at www.macmillan.com.au or go directly to www.macmillanlibrary.com.au

Associated companies and representatives throughout the world.

Library of Congress Cataloging-in-Publication Data

Chapman, Garry.
  Coffee / Garry Chapman and Gary Hodges.
    p. cm. — (World commodities)
  Includes index.
  ISBN 978-1-59920-584-7 (library binding)
  1. Coffee industry—Juvenile literature. 2. Coffee—Juvenile literature. I. Hodges, Gary. II. Title.
  HD9199.A2C52 2011
  338.1'7373—dc22
                                        2010007305

Publisher: Carmel Heron   Designer: Ivan Finnegan (cover and text)
Commissioning Editor: Niki Horin   Page Layout: Ivan Finnegan
Managing Editor: Vanessa Lanaway   Photo Researcher: Lesya Bryndzia (management: Debbie Gallagher)
Editor: Laura Jeanne Gobal   Illustrators: Andy Craig and Nives Porcellato, 15, 25; Alan Laver, 17
Proofreader: Kirstie Innes-Will   Production Controller: Vanessa Johnson

Manufactured in the United States of America by Corporate Graphics, Minnesota.
052010

Acknowledgments
The author and the publisher are grateful to the following for permission to reproduce copyright material:

Front cover photograph of coffee beans: 123RF/Serghei Starus

Bloomberg via Getty Images/Jeff Holt, **21**, /Claire Leow, **24**, /Michael Tsegaye, **18**; Corbis, **5**, /Andy Aitchison, **23**, /Paulo Fridman, **9** (top), /Janet Jarman, **11** (bottom); Getty Images/AFP/Alessandro Abbonizio, **26**, /AFP/Jose Cendon, **29**, /AFP/MauricioLima, **14**, /Apic, **8** (top), /Dorling Kindersley, **4** (iron ore), /Rob Melnychuk, **29**, /Time Life Pictures/Leonard Mccombe, **20**; iStockphoto/Ajay Bhaskar, **27**, /Kelly Cline, **11** (top), /Scott Griessel, **7**, /Lasse Kristensen, **13** (2nd bottom), /Aga & Miko Materne, **13** (bottom), /newphotoservice, **13** (2nd top); Jasper Coffee, **19** (right); Photolibrary/Norman Hollands, **10** (bottom), /North Wind Picture Archives, **8** (bottom); Shutterstock/Forest Badger, **4** (oil), /Drozdowski, **12**, /Gianluca Figliola Fantini, **11** (middle), /IDAL, **4** (wheat), /ikopylov, **13** (top), /kgelati, **9** (bottom), /VenkateshMurthy, **10** (top), /Worldpics, **4** (coal), /yykkaa, **4** (sugar), /Magdalena Zurawska, **4** (coffee); UN Photo/Jerry Frank, **10** (middle).

While every care has been taken to trace and acknowledge copyright, the publisher tenders their apologies for any accidental infringement where copyright has proved untraceable. Where the attempt has been unsuccessful, the publisher welcomes information that would redress the situation.

Please note: At the time of printing, the Internet addresses appearing in this book were correct. Owing to the dynamic nature of the Internet, however, we cannot guarantee that all of these addresses will remain correct.

This series is for my father, Ron Chapman, with gratitude. – Garry Chapman
This series is dedicated to the memory of Jean and Alex Ross, as well as my immediate family of Sue, Hannah and Jessica,
my parents, Jim and Val, and my brother Leigh. – Gary Hodges

Contents

Glossary Words

When a word is printed in **bold**, you can look up its meaning in the Glossary on page 31.

What Is a World Commodity?

A commodity is any product for which someone is willing to pay money. A world commodity is a product that is traded across the world.

The World's Most Widely Traded Commodities

Many of the world's most widely traded commodities are **agricultural** products, such as coffee, sugar, and wheat, or **natural resources**, such as coal, iron ore, and oil. These commodities are produced in large amounts by people around the world.

Coal, coffee, iron ore, oil, sugar, and wheat are important commodities traded around the world.

Commodities and the World's Economy

Whenever the world's **demand** for a commodity increases or decreases, the price of this commodity goes up or down by the same amount everywhere. Prices usually vary from day to day. The daily trade in world commodities plays a key role in the state of the world's **economy**.

MORE ABOUT...
The Quality of Commodities

When people, businesses, or countries buy a commodity, they assume that its quality will be consistent. Oil is an example of a commodity. When people trade in oil, all barrels of oil are considered to be of the same quality regardless of where they come from.

Coffee Is a Commodity

Coffee is one of the world's most popular drinks. It is also the world's leading agricultural commodity.

Where Does Coffee Come From?

Coffee comes from coffee berries, which grow on small trees. Coffee berries are harvested for their beans, which are then roasted to produce the special flavors and **aromas** that coffee drinkers enjoy so much. The two most common coffee trees are *Coffea robusta* and *Coffea arabica*.

Coffee Varieties and Preparation Styles

Today, coffee drinkers may select from a wide range of coffee varieties and preparation styles. These range from inexpensive instant coffee to special blends expertly prepared by a **barista**.

Robusta coffee is often used in cheaper commercial blends of coffee. It has a more bitter taste and less flavor than coffee made from arabica beans. It also contains more of the **stimulant** known as caffeine than arabica coffee does.

Millions of people all over the world start their day with a cup of coffee.

Where Is Coffee Grown and Where Is It Consumed?

Coffee is grown in more than 50 countries worldwide by about 25 million growers. It is consumed by people all over the world.

Growing Coffee

Coffee grows in tropical parts of Asia, Africa, and Latin America. It needs a rainy season, during which the trees flower, and a longer, relatively dry season, during which the berries develop and are harvested. There are two main types of coffee – *Coffea arabica* and *Coffea robusta*.

COMPARING *COFFEA ROBUSTA* AND *COFFEA ARABICA*

	Coffea arabica	*Coffea robusta*
Location	Arabian Peninsula, Asia, Brazil, the Caribbean, Central America, Colombia, East Africa, Peru	Brazil, Indonesia, Central and West Africa, Vietnam
Type of Farm	Small, family-run farms	Large plantations
Terrain	Mountainous rain forest, richer soil	Flat, closer to sea level, poorer soil
Climate	Often grown in the shade, in regions with high rainfall	Often grown in sunny, drier regions
Hardiness	More prone to disease	More resistant to disease
Harvesting Method	Hand-picked	By machine
Type of Coffee	Often used in specialist coffee	Often used in instant coffee
Caffeine Level	Approximately 1 percent	Approximately 2 percent
Taste	More flavorsome	More bitter

Regional Differences

Coffee beans from different regions each have their own distinctive flavors and aromas. These differences are caused by many factors, including **altitude**, climate, and soil conditions.

Coffee Consumption

Coffee is consumed all over the world. The United States, where coffee is very popular, **imports** more coffee than any other country. Germany and Japan also import large amounts of coffee.

Many people enjoy drinking coffee with friends.

THE WORLD'S MAJOR COFFEE CONSUMERS (2009)

Country	Amount of Coffee Consumed Per Person, Per Year (pounds / kg)
Finland	27.8 lb (12.6 kg)
Switzerland	20.1 lb (9.1 kg)
Norway	19.8 lb (9.0 kg)
Sweden	18.3 lb (8.3 kg)
Iceland	18.3 lb (8.3 kg)

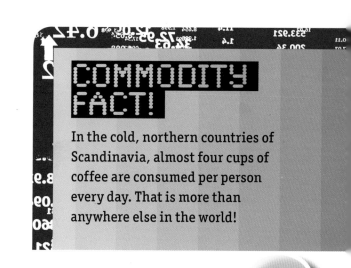

COMMODITY FACT!

In the cold, northern countries of Scandinavia, almost four cups of coffee are consumed per person every day. That is more than anywhere else in the world!

Timeline: **The History of Coffee**

Humans first drank coffee more than 1,000 years ago. Since then, it has been traded all over the world, making it a highly valued commodity.

about A.D. 850
Coffee is first consumed when the *Coffea arabica* plant is discovered in the highlands of Ethiopia.

about 1400
Many pilgrims visit Mecca, in present-day Saudi Arabia. At coffeehouses, they sip coffee while enjoying entertainment and conversation.

1616
Coffee plants smuggled from Aden, in Yemen, are successfully grown in Dutch **colonies** elsewhere. For the first time, coffee is grown outside an Arab country.

An early coffee machine being used in a Parisian coffeehouse in 1856.

A.D. 850

about 1000
The coffee trade begins. Coffee beans are shipped from the port of Mocha to Yemen and elsewhere on the Arabian Peninsula, where they are roasted and brewed for the first time.

about 1600
Arabian traders introduce coffee to Europe via the Italian port of Venice. Venetian merchants charge the wealthy high prices for the privilege of drinking coffee.

about 1700
Coffeehouses become common across Europe. Much of the coffee consumed is imported by the Dutch from their colonies in Indonesia.

1715
In a Paris greenhouse, a coffee tree owned by Louis XIV bears fruit. A seedling from this tree is used to establish coffee plantations in France's Caribbean colonies. Slaves are transported from Africa to work on these plantations.

Local workers harvesting coffee in Costa Rica in the 1800s.

1727
Coffee is smuggled into Brazil from French Guiana. So much coffee is grown in Brazil that its price plummets. Soon, everyone in Europe can afford to drink coffee.

Brazil is one of the main coffee-growing countries.

about 1970
A "coffee culture" is established throughout Europe, the United States, Australia, Japan, and other parts of the industrialized world. Coffeehouses grow in popularity.

1999
Vietnam triples the amount of coffee it **exported** in 1995 to become the world's leading producer of robusta coffee.

A.D. 2010

1988
The first coffee certified by Fairtrade is produced. Many socially conscious coffee drinkers will only buy coffee produced by growers who are paid a fair price for it.

2010
More than 100 million people worldwide rely on the production of coffee as their main source of income.

1893
Coffee plants from Brazil are used to establish plantations in East Africa, bringing coffee back to its birthplace.

Today's cafés and coffeehouses serve high-quality coffee sourced from different countries.

about 1780
Coffeehouses are established in the United States and many people there start drinking coffee.

How Is Coffee Made?

When coffee berries are ripe, they are harvested, sorted, and dried. Their beans are then roasted to bring out the flavor of the coffee.

Bearing Fruit

Coffee trees flower and bear fruit in the form of berries. As the berries ripen, they change color from green to yellow and finally to red. Two seeds known as coffee beans can be found inside each berry.

Harvesting

On small family farms in hilly terrain, workers handpick the berries. Larger plantations on flat ground, such as those found in Brazil and Vietnam, are more likely to use machinery to harvest the berries.

Sorting

In a factory, the berries are sorted by ripeness. The flesh is removed, leaving a slimy pulp around the beans. The berries are then allowed to **ferment**. This makes the pulp easy to wash off with water.

Storage

The roasted beans are stored in airtight containers and kept cool. This ensures their freshness and flavor. They are now ready to be sold to consumers.

Roasting

The coffee beans are roasted. They transform during the roasting process, becoming smaller and changing in color to dark brown. At just over 392°F (200°C), the beans release an oil called caffeol. It lightly coats the beans, giving the coffee its flavor and aroma.

Drying, Grading, and Bagging

The pulp-free, green coffee beans are dried in the sun. The dried beans are sent to a hulling mill, where the dry outer skin is removed. The beans are sorted, graded, and bagged according to size. They are then sold to roasters.

Preparing Coffee for Consumption

Soon after the roasting process, the coffee beans are sold to **consumers**. They remain fresh for up to one month.

Grinding

Roasted coffee beans are ground before the coffee is brewed. To enjoy the best flavor, coffee should be consumed immediately after the beans have been ground. There are several ways to grind coffee beans. The ground beans can be very fine, quite coarse, or anywhere in between.

Coffee grinders, such as this hand-operated model, are used to grind roasted coffee beans.

Brewing

Coffee can be brewed using different methods, some of which are described in the table below.

Serving

Once coffee has been brewed, it can be served in different ways. We can:

- add milk or cream (adding steamed milk will make a café latté and adding milk froth will make a cappuccino)
- add sugar or an artificial sweetener
- add milk and ice cream to make iced coffee
- drink it without adding anything (often referred to as black coffee)

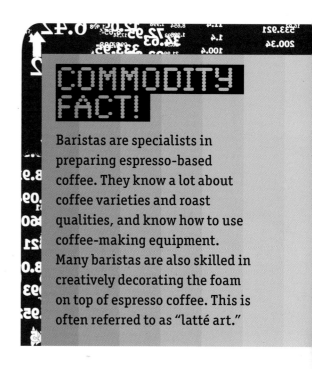

COMMODITY FACT!

Baristas are specialists in preparing espresso-based coffee. They know a lot about coffee varieties and roast qualities, and know how to use coffee-making equipment. Many baristas are also skilled in creatively decorating the foam on top of espresso coffee. This is often referred to as "latté art."

COFFEE BREWING STYLES

Brewing Style		Brewing Method
Turkish Coffee		Roasted coffee beans are crushed into a very fine powder and added to water. The mixture is then boiled to make a very strong coffee.
Percolated Coffee		Boiling water is passed through ground coffee beans held in a metal basket. The water absorbs the oils which give the coffee its flavor and aroma.
French Press Coffee		Ground coffee beans and boiling water are brewed in a coffee pot before a plunger is depressed to separate the grounds from the drink.
Espresso Coffee		Hot water is forced through tightly packed ground coffee at high pressure to make espresso.

The Coffee Trade

Coffee is the second-most-traded commodity in the world, behind only oil. The coffee trade involves approximately 50 countries, 25 million growers, and 27 million acres (11 million ha) of land.

Price Variations and Deregulation

Since the 1880s, the world price of coffee has experienced many highs and lows, which is normal for an agricultural commodity. Variations in price over time are a feature of the **boom and bust cycle**.

Between 1962 and 1989, the price of coffee remained relatively stable, largely due to a series of International Coffee Agreements. These agreements, which set limits on the amount of coffee that could be imported, collapsed when **deregulation** was introduced. The price of coffee often rose and then fell in this deregulated environment.

Coffee trading takes place every day on busy trading floors, such as the Brazilian Mercantile and Futures Exchange (BM&F) in São Paulo.

Exchanges

An exchange is a place where commodities, such as coffee, are bought and sold. At an exchange, coffee is bought and sold in both the futures market and spot market.

The Futures Market

The futures market is where buyers and sellers agree on a specific price for shipments of coffee in the future. Buying coffee in this way will protect both the buyer and seller from price variations, which may occur in the months ahead. Regardless of whether the world price of coffee rises or falls, the coffee will change hands at the price agreed on when the contract was signed.

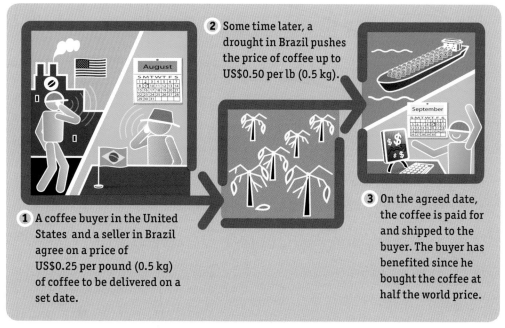

1. A coffee buyer in the United States and a seller in Brazil agree on a price of US$0.25 per pound (0.5 kg) of coffee to be delivered on a set date.

2. Some time later, a drought in Brazil pushes the price of coffee up to US$0.50 per lb (0.5 kg).

3. On the agreed date, the coffee is paid for and shipped to the buyer. The buyer has benefited since he bought the coffee at half the world price.

The futures trading of coffee takes place in three main stages. The coffee buyer is agreeing to buy coffee at a future date for a set price.

The Spot Market

The spot market is where buyers and sellers agree on a price for the immediate exchange of shipments of coffee. As soon as the coffee is bought, it changes hands.

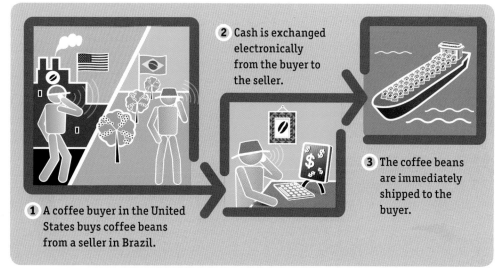

1. A coffee buyer in the United States buys coffee beans from a seller in Brazil.

2. Cash is exchanged electronically from the buyer to the seller.

3. The coffee beans are immediately shipped to the buyer.

The spot trading of coffee is a simple transaction between a coffee grower and a coffee buyer that takes place in three main stages.

Supply and Demand

The coffee trade is determined by **supply** and demand. When **consumers** are eager to buy the commodity, the demand for coffee increases. Consumers rely on producers to supply it.

Factors Affecting Supply

There are many factors affecting the supply of coffee.
- The world price of coffee affects whether growers can afford to grow it.
- Local weather conditions can affect how well coffee crops grow.
- The transportation systems in and from coffee-growing countries determines whether coffee can reach its export markets.

Factors Affecting Demand

Similarly, there are many factors affecting the demand for coffee.
- Coffee-consuming countries might import less coffee if the world price is too high.
- The population of coffee-drinking countries affects how many people demand coffee.
- Consumers' view of coffee and its production can affect how much coffee they drink.

THE WORLD'S TOP EXPORTERS AND IMPORTERS OF COFFEE (2008–2009)

Exporter	Amount of Coffee Exported	Importer	Amount of Coffee Imported
Brazil	2,078,138 tons (1,889,216 t)	United States	1,584,924 tons (1,440,840 t)
Vietnam	1,157,698 tons (1,052,453 t)	Germany	1,303,368 tons (1,184,880 t)
Colombia	634,018 tons (576,380 t)	Italy	532,620 tons (484,200 t)
Indonesia	394,433 tons (358,575 t)	Japan	482,526 tons (438,660 t)
Peru	251,781 tons (228,892 t)	Belgium	430,716 tons (391,560 t)

Price Variations

When the global demand for coffee is greater than its supply, the price of coffee increases. In the same way, when the supply of coffee is greater than the demand for it, the world coffee price falls.

THE RISE AND FALL OF THE WORLD PRICE OF COFFEE

1998
Coffee growers sell their **surplus** stock at a high price before coffee supplies decrease.

2007
Crop shortages in key coffee-producing countries cause the price of coffee to rise.

2004–2005
There is increased consumer demand for coffee, particularly from Asia. Coffee crops fail in Brazil. The price of coffee rises.

The world price of coffee experiences highs and lows over time. Events around the world influence the supply of and demand for the commodity, which changes the price.

2008
Coffee production declines despite strong international demand for coffee. The price of coffee rises.

US cents per pound (0.5 kg)

123.3
106.1
88.9
71.7
54.5
37.3
20.1
0

1998 1999 2000 2001 2002 2003 2004 2005 2006 2007 2008
Year

1999
There is a global oversupply of coffee. Vietnam contributes to this problem by becoming a major producer of coffee. The price of coffee falls.

2002
Coffee is oversupplied again during a period of slowing demand. The price of coffee falls.

2005–2006
Vietnam continues to dominate the market as a coffee producer. The price of coffee falls.

17

Codes of Practice

Codes of practice govern the way most commodities are traded internationally. The purpose of these codes is to ensure growers are paid a fair amount, allowing them to maintain a reasonable standard of living, in exchange for their coffee.

International Coffee Agreements

Between 1962 and 1989, the International Coffee Organization (ICO) promoted International Coffee Agreements to ensure a fairer deal for coffee growers. Similar agreements are still negotiated by the ICO today. However, due to deregulation in 1989, those involved in the coffee trade are not bound to these agreements.

The coffee trade is still partially coordinated by the ICO, which recommends guidelines and sets standards on important issues, such as coffee quality, marketing, and **sustainability**.

Deregulation has made it harder for many coffee growers to sell their coffee at a fair price. It has allowed large roasting companies to dominate the coffee trade and limit the amount paid to growers.

Fairtrade Labelling Organizations International

There are a number of organizations which, like the ICO, aim to set basic standards for the coffee trade. Fairtrade Labelling Organizations International (FLO) is one of them.

Fairtrade Certification

Fairtrade certification ensures that products are made and sold in a socially, environmentally, and economically responsible way. For coffee to be certified and bear the Fairtrade mark:

- a minimum fair price must be paid for washed arabica beans
- an additional sum of money must be paid to the farmer for social, economic, and environmental development within their business and communities
- long-term contracts of up to 10 years must be negotiated with growers

The Fairtrade logo is visible on the packaging used by **ethical** roasters. By choosing this coffee, the buyer too is acting ethically.

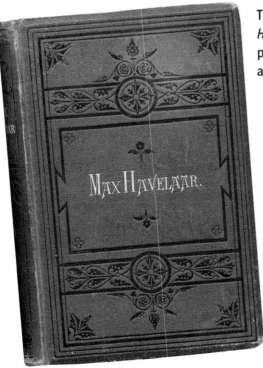

The novel *Max Havelaar* was first published in 1860 and is still in print.

MORE ABOUT...

Fairtrade Labelling Organizations International

FLO is based on the ideals of Max Havelaar, a character from an 1860 Dutch novel of the same name, set in Indonesia. Havelaar fought against the unfair laws and taxes that the Dutch colonial government imposed on coffee growers. The novel's success raised awareness about the conditions of coffee growers, led to the development of Fairtrade, and helped give coffee growers a better deal.

International Politics and Coffee

Coffee is a very valuable commodity. It is important to the economies of many **developing countries**. The leaders of major coffee-producing countries, such as Brazil and Vietnam, often base their political decisions on protecting the coffee industry in the global market.

Brazil in the 1930s

Since the founding of the Brazilian republic in 1889, Brazil's economy has relied heavily on the coffee industry. However, in 1929, the Wall Street stock market crash in New York sent the price of coffee plummeting to about one-tenth of its price a year earlier. To protect Brazil against future falls in the price of coffee, then President Getúlio Vargas set up the National Coffee Committee in 1931. The committee adopted a policy that would see excess coffee being purchased and burned to limit the supply to the international market.

Under President Vargas's (front right) leadership, the Brazilian government kept excess coffee to prevent it from reaching the market and lowering the price of coffee.

Vietnam in the 1990s

By the mid-1990s, the United States had lifted the trade sanctions, or penalties, it had placed on Vietnam following the Vietnam War. Coffee had been a major source of income for Vietnam, but the war and sanctions had interrupted its production and prevented its sale, leaving the country in debt. The **World Bank** helped Vietnam restart its coffee industry. As coffee sales soared, the country was soon able to reduce its large debts. The United States government was supportive of the Vietnamese coffee industry because it offered an alternative to the increasing number of **socialist** coffee-producing countries in Latin America.

MORE ABOUT...

Coffee and Vietnam's Montagnard People

The rise of the coffee industry in Vietnam has made life very difficult for the **indigenous** Montagnard people in Vietnam's central highlands. Their traditional lands are now home to coffee plantations. The Montagnards have been forced to move to infertile land, where they struggle to grow crops.

The world price of robusta coffee has dropped due to supplies from Vietnamese coffee growers increasing each year.

21

Environmental Issues and Coffee

The coffee industry faces a number of environmental challenges. How the commodity is grown can have a negative impact on the land.

Sunlight versus Shade

Many coffee growers experience pressure from buyers to grow their coffee in direct sunlight. Although this produces greater **yields**, it also forces growers to clear forested land. This leaves fewer trees available to absorb harmful carbon dioxide from the air and turn it into precious oxygen. It also leaves birds with fewer trees to take shelter in. Furthermore, sun-ripened coffee crops usually need chemical fertilizers and pesticides, which can lead to the contamination of surrounding soil and water.

SUN-GROWN OR SHADE-GROWN COFFEE?

	Sun-grown	Shade-grown
Coffee Type	Robusta	Arabica
Terrain	Flat	Hilly
Yield	Large	Small
Farming Method	Fertilizers and pesticides	**Organic**
Environmental Impact	High	Low
Bird Friendly	No	Yes
Harvesting Method	By machine	Hand-picked

Organic Coffee

Organic coffee growers improve the soil by using compost rather than chemical fertilizers or pesticides. Organic coffee usually brings a higher price from roasters. More growers, including growers in some parts of Brazil, are trying to grow organic coffee which is certified. It takes three years for a grower's crop to be certified as organic. Inspections then occur every year to ensure that strict environmental standards are maintained.

Crop Rotation

Crop rotation is a farming method in which different crops are grown in the same field at different times. This helps nourish the soil and prevent crop diseases. In coffee plantations that use crop rotation, coffee crops are grown for a period, then replaced by vegetables, legumes, or small fruit trees for a year. Coffee crops can then be planted once more. This limits the amount of coffee that can be produced but maintains the long-term productivity of the land, so that growing coffee is sustainable.

> *"In the beginning, my reason to start organic production was because of the market, but my mind has been changed over the past couple [of] years as I've seen the benefits to the land and environment. I'm pleased that I am doing something good for the environment."*
>
> **A grower in Brazil**
> (Source: www.shareagfoundation.org/newsletters/2007-November-Newsletter.pdf)

Kulika is a program that runs sustainable, organic agricultural training programs in Uganda. In the Kamuli district, young coffee seedlings are being grown in a nursery, protected from the harsh sunlight.

23

Social Issues and Coffee

Social issues exist in the coffee industry because most coffee is grown in developing countries, where many people live near or below the **poverty line**. Variations in global supply and demand can have a strong impact on these communities.

Low-income Coffee Growers

More than 25 million growers around the world rely on the coffee industry for a living. Even when there is a good harvest, many growers are so poorly paid for their crops that looking after their families is a struggle. If a crisis occurs and they cannot sell their coffee, the impact could be so crippling that some growers might be forced to leave their farms and move to the city in search of other work.

Vietnamese Coffee in the 1990s

Coffee growers may experience great hardships because of factors beyond their control. For example, in the late 1980s, coffee growers from Latin America had little trouble selling their coffee to a world in which the "coffee culture" was developing. However, in the 1990s, Vietnam entered the coffee trade, producing large amounts of coffee and selling it cheaply to importers. As a result, the world suddenly had a surplus of coffee. The cheap Vietnamese coffee sold quickly, leaving other growers unable to sell their coffee for what it was worth. The competition from Vietnam plunged coffee-growing communities elsewhere into poverty.

When large amounts of inexpensive Vietnamese coffee flooded the world market in the 1990s, many growers elsewhere suffered hardship.

Taking Advantage of Growers

Roasting companies often use an agent, or middleman, to negotiate a price with a grower. For various reasons, such as lack of education, the need for money or feeling pressured by the middleman, the grower is likely to accept a price which is too low. The middleman then sells the coffee to the roasting company at a higher price and makes a large profit.

One solution to this problem is the formation of **cooperatives**. The coffee grown belongs to the cooperative, which only agrees to sell it to those who will pay a fair price for it. The profits are then shared equally among all members. Profits may be used to get better access to healthcare and education, and to get trained in more productive farming techniques.

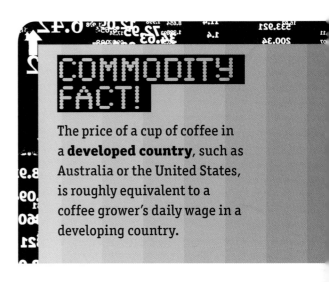

COMMODITY FACT!

The price of a cup of coffee in a **developed country**, such as Australia or the United States, is roughly equivalent to a coffee grower's daily wage in a developing country.

Consumer Support

Consumers can take a stand against the social issues facing growers by purchasing only ethically sourced coffee. Large, multinational coffeehouses and fast-food chains have responded to public pressure by serving only coffee for which growers have received fair prices.

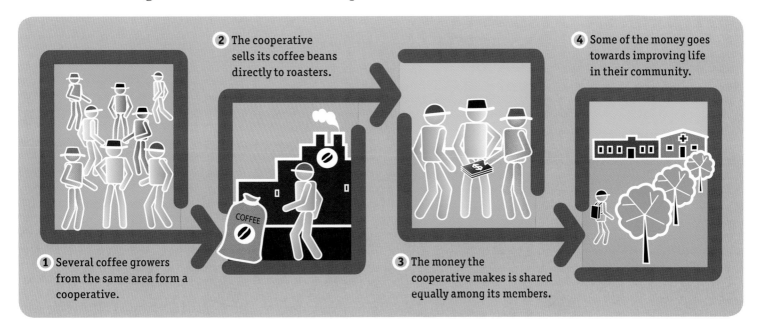

1 Several coffee growers from the same area form a cooperative.

2 The cooperative sells its coffee beans directly to roasters.

3 The money the cooperative makes is shared equally among its members.

4 Some of the money goes towards improving life in their community.

Coffee cooperatives can help growers make their farming methods more sustainable.

Is the Coffee Industry Sustainable?

To sustain something is to keep it going for a very long time. There are three aspects to keeping the coffee industry sustainable: making sure coffee-growing communities can survive, protecting the environment in which coffee is grown, and maintaining the demand for coffee.

Sustainable Coffee-growing Communities

Many of the world's coffee growers are very poor and, often, coffee is their only source of income. They are usually paid low prices by the large roasting companies that buy their coffee beans. As a result, many cannot afford proper healthcare or education for their children. Events beyond their control, such as wild weather or changes in the world market, can bring great hardship to these growers.

Community-based Cooperatives

One way to improve conditions for coffee growers is to form a cooperative. Cooperatives negotiate directly with roasting companies and are able to take a stand against low prices. In addition to sharing the profits equally among the growers, cooperatives also put a percentage of their income toward supporting and caring for the coffee-growing community. Certified coffee is often purchased from cooperatives.

Consumers are very important in the fight against unfair trading practices. By purchasing only ethically sourced coffee, they can force roasters and coffeehouses to change their trading practices.

DUE TO **YOUR** DEMAND

OUR COFFEE IS NOW **100%** FAIRTRADE

Protecting the Environment

If growers were paid a fair price for their coffee, they would not have to grow as much coffee to make enough money to live on. This means less land would have to be cleared, and they could also afford to practice sustainable farming. They could plant shade trees and cut back on the use of chemical fertilizers and pesticides. In this way, they would not only be protecting the environment, but they would also be producing high-quality, shade-grown, organic coffee. Although this could result in slightly higher coffee prices for consumers, they would all benefit from an improved product and a healthier environment.

Many coffee drinkers are prepared to pay a little more for high-quality, shade-grown, organic coffee.

Maintaining the Demand for Coffee

Most consumers know that the best way to guarantee an ongoing supply of high-quality coffee is to support sustainable coffee growers by buying their coffee. As the demand for certified organic coffee increases, more growers will be encouraged to switch to sustainable farming.

MORE ABOUT...
Making Money from Farming

Coffee growers can also add to their income by developing other ways of making money while still growing coffee. They can grow fruit and vegetables, in addition to coffee, or keep livestock, such as pigs or chickens, which can be sold.

27

The Future of the Coffee Industry

The future of the coffee industry will be determined by the ability of coffee growers to continue producing a quality product. To do this, they must receive support from **consumers** and be paid fairly for their crops.

A Return to Price Regulation

The International Coffee Organization (ICO) provided security for coffee growers through negotiated International Coffee Agreements until 1989, when deregulation was introduced. These agreements set **quotas** on exports and imports to help stabilize coffee prices. A return to such price regulation would benefit many growers. However, to be effective, it would also require support from major coffee roasters and retailers, financial institutions such as the World Bank, and the governments of importing and exporting countries.

The support of organizations such as the World Bank will be needed if international coffee agreements are to be effective. Here, the former president of the World Bank, Paul Wolfowitz (far right), visits a coffee-washing station in Rwanda.

Certification Offers Hope

Increasing consumer confidence in coffee certified by organizations such as Fairtrade and the Rainforest Alliance also offers hope to growers in search of a better deal. As more consumers buy certified coffee, coffee-growing cooperatives receive greater financial support. This, in turn, may encourage growers to consider organic farming, planting coffee trees in the shade, and reducing the use of chemical fertilizers and pesticides.

Smart Coffee Consumers

Consumers understand that by paying a higher price for certified coffee, they support the growers who produce it, and they receive a better product in return. If consumers become informed about the conditions under which their coffee is grown, it is likely they will buy coffee only from companies that do not take advantage of coffee growers.

Well-informed consumers understand that choosing certified coffee supports the growers who produce it.

More Choices for Coffee Consumers

The future looks bright for coffee consumers. They can now purchase coffee that satisfies their personal tastes as well as their ethical standards. They can obtain coffee from any of the world's best growing regions and drink it in many different ways.

MORE ABOUT...
The Informed Coffee Drinker

Over the past ten years, as the demand for high-quality coffee has grown, the espresso machine has become a very popular appliance in many homes. Coffee drinkers now know more about the flavors and aromas that can be obtained from different varieties and blends. They are comfortable with paying higher prices for the improved taste that high-quality coffee and an espresso machine provide.

Find Out More

Web Sites for Further Information

- ### The coffee plant
Learn more about the plants which produce coffee beans.
www.coffeeresearch.org/coffee/coffeeplant.htm

- ### The story of coffee
Learn more about the history of coffee.
www.ico.org/coffee_story.asp

- ### Coffee trading defined and explained
Learn more about how shifts in supply and demand affect the trade in coffee.
www.tradertech.com/information/coffeetrading.asp

- ### Fairtrade Labelling Organizations International
Learn more about the Fairtrade movement and where to purchase Fairtrade products.
www.fairtrade.net/

Focus Questions

These questions might help you think about some of the issues raised in this book.

- What are the advantages and disadvantages of reintroducing the International Coffee Agreements?

- What can coffee growers do to increase their income from growing coffee?

- Would you be willing to pay more for coffee if you knew the growers would be paid a fair price?

- Can the use of chemical fertilizers and pesticides in the coffee industry be justified?

Glossary

agricultural	related to farming or used for farming
altitude	height above sea level
aromas	strong, pleasant smells
barista	a person who is skilled at making espresso coffee
boom and bust cycle	an established economic trend where prices rise and fall
colonies	countries which have been settled and are governed by a more powerful country
cooperatives	organizations which are owned and managed by the people who work in them, for their mutual benefit
demand	the amount of a product consumers want to buy
deregulation	when rules and regulations governing the trade of a commodity are removed in order to improve efficiency in markets and organizations
developed country	a country that is very industrialized
developing countries	countries in the early stages of becoming industrialized
economy	a system that organizes the production, distribution, and exchange of goods and services, as well as incomes
ethical	relating to beliefs about what is right or wrong
exported	sold or sent to another country
ferment	to go through a chemical change caused by living organisms, such as bacteria
imports	products which are bought or brought in from another country; or the action of buying and bringing a product into a country
indigenous	naturally existing or belonging to a particular region or country
natural resources	the naturally occurring, useful wealth of a region or country, such as land, forests, coal, oil, gas, and water
organic	grown without the use of chemical fertilizers or pesticides
poverty line	the lowest level of income which is needed for a person to have a basic standard of living
quotas	limits on the amount of certain commodities which can be imported
socialist	relating to socialism, an economic theory that proposes public ownership and administration of all resources
stimulant	a substance which makes the body or mind more active
supply	the amount of a product that producers are able to sell
surplus	an amount which is more than is needed
sustainability	the ability to continue over a period of time
terrain	an area of land and its natural features
World Bank	an international financial institution which loans money and provides advice to developing countries
yields	produces; or the amounts produced

Index